NATIONAL GEOGRAPHIC **OUR WORLD**

# Mouse Deer
# in the Rain Forest

## A Folktale from Indonesia

Retold by Anna Olivia

NATIONAL
GEOGRAPHIC
LEARNING

CENGAGE
Learning

One afternoon in the rain forest,
Mouse Deer is swimming in the river.
As he swims he sings,
   "I am smart. Everyone can see.
   You can try, but you can't catch me!"

Suddenly, Tiger comes through the trees.
"Why are you in the water?" asks Tiger.
"Because I'm hot," says Mouse Deer.

3

"I am not hot," says Tiger. "But I am hungry!"

Mouse Deer says, "If you don't eat me, you can have the king's soup."

Mouse Deer points to a puddle in the sand.

"Why is the king's soup brown?"
asks Tiger.

"Because it's made of chocolate,"
says Mouse Deer.

"Chocolate!" says Tiger. "I love chocolate!"

Tiger takes a big drink of the puddle.
"Yuck!" says Tiger. "You tricked me! It's mud!"
Mouse Deer runs away.

Tiger chases Mouse Deer through the rain forest.

"Ha!" says Mouse Deer. "You can't catch me!"

But Tiger is fast and hungry. He catches little Mouse Deer under a tall tree.

Mouse Deer says, "If you don't eat me, you can have that drum!"

"Why is the drum in the tree?" asks Tiger.

"Because it's the king's drum," says Mouse Deer. "I put it there to protect it."

"The king's drum must make beautiful music," says Tiger.
"I want it!"
Tiger climbs up the tree and takes the drum.
But the drum is really a hornet's hive!

The hornets chase Tiger through the rain forest.
Tiger runs to the river and jumps in.

Mouse Deer sees Tiger is okay.
Then he sings,
   "I am smart. Now Tiger can see.
   He can try, but he can't catch me!"

Tiger never bothers Mouse Deer again.

# Facts About Rain Forest Animals

Mouse Deer and Tiger live in the rain forest in Indonesia. Indonesia has many islands and more unique wildlife than any other country. Here are some other animals that live in the Indonesian rain forest.

**Animal:** Orangutan
**Fun Fact:** Orangutans make and sleep in a new nest in the trees each night.

**Animal:** Palm Civet
**Fun Fact:** Civets make a terrible smell to keep away animals that want to eat them.

**Animal:** Komodo Dragon
**Fun Fact:** The Komodo dragon is the biggest lizard in the world.

**Animal:**
Pygmy Tarsier
**Fun Fact:**
Tarsiers can't move their eyes, so they have to move their heads to see things around them.

**Animal:** Sumatran Rhinoceros
**Fun Fact:** The Sumatran Rhino eats only plants and no meat.

**Animal:**
Stick Insects
**Fun Fact:** The color of some stick insects changes at night to make it harder to see them.

# **Fun with** Rain Forests

What is the word for each thing in the picture?

rain forest     mud     river     sand

1. __rain forest__

2. _____

3. _____

4. _____

Which things are in a rain forest? Circle them.

ice

trees

bird

whale

snow

river

insect

camel

leaf

What else is in a rain forest? Draw pictures or write words. Use a bilingual dictionary if necessary.

# Glossary

**chases** runs after something to try to catch it

**chocolate** a kind of food that is usually brown and sweet

**hornets** flying insects that sting

**king** a man who rules a country

**lizard** a type of animal called a reptile, with a long body, four legs, and a tail

**music** sound made by singing and playing instruments

**puddle** a small bit of water in one place